HANN.^...

1 Samuel 1 and

NTRODUCTION

Hannah was the wife of a dedicated man of God and the mother of a great prophet. Yet her life was not an easy one. She went through difficult personal circumstances with which many of us would sympathize today.

1 Hannah's Hurt: our response to suffering.

2 Hannah's Prayer: prayer without pretending.

3 Hannah's Family: loving God *and* our families.

To get a feel for Hannah's situation, four people could read the first part of the study (1 Samuel 1) taking the parts of narrator, Elkanah, Hannah and Eli.

A IM

That every member of the group may go away with the reassurance that, like Hannah, God knows their deepest needs and hears their prayers.

Hannah's Hurt

Read 1 Samuel 1:1-8. Hannah experiences the social stigma of child-lessness, one of the greatest tragedies to befall a Hebrew woman. The passage raises the question of our response to suffering.

1   *Verses 1-8* Put yourself in Hannah's shoes. What sort of emotions would you be experiencing? List them and then discuss.

2   *Verse 5* 'The Lord had kept her from having children.' Is this how you understand childlessness? Have members of the group experienced problems conceiving a family? How real was God during those hard times?

3   Read Philippians 4:1-13. The apostle Paul tells us that God can help us cope with any situation. Does this mean we should just accept our lot in life or, like Hannah, pray for change? How would you help someone for whom the answer to that prayer seems to be 'no' or 'not yet'?

Hannah's Prayer

Read 1 Samuel 1:9-18. Hannah prays in desperation. We can learn from her about honest prayer and its results.

1 *Verse 9* 'Hannah cried bitterly as she prayed to the Lord.'

When have you been at rock-bottom? Did you, like Hannah, cry out to the Lord?

2 *Verses 13-16* Hannah's troubles were not over. She spent so long in prayer Eli thought she was drunk. Do we ever miss the chance to help people in great need because we misread their actions?

3 *Verse 18* Note the effect of Hannah's prayer: 'Then she went away and was no longer sad.' She had talked to the Lord and he had reassured her. What can we learn from Hannah's prayer?

Discuss

Many people turn to God only in times of crisis such as accident, death and so on. How do we answer them when they say God did not listen?

Hannah's Family

Read 1 Samuel 1:19-28 and 2:11-21. Hannah gives birth to Samuel and takes him to the temple. The story raises questions of how we combine love for God with love for our families.

1 *Verse 22* How did Hannah fulfil her promises to God? Was Hannah's attitude to God a healthy one? How do we rate when it comes to putting aside time for:

❑ church activities?

❑ family life?

2 Do you find one always takes precedence, or do you make a conscious effort to balance the two?

3 *Verse 23* Hannah seems to have had a good relationship with her husband. Do you find it easy to share your Christian life with your partner or with close friends?

4 *Verses 27-28* Christians dedicate their children to the Lord in different ways. What would be a contemporary equivalent of Hannah's actions?

Share with the group any experiences of God asking you to make sacrifices in your family life.

Discuss

Should Christian parents, and others with the care of children, feel they have failed if children grow up and do not follow Christ?

Prayer

As a group, read 1 Samuel 2:1-10 in chorus. Lead into a time of prayer, thinking particularly of personal needs and circumstances among group members which have been shared during the study.

RUTH

Ruth 1-4

NTRODUCTION

Ruth is a well-known Old Testament figure, yet many aspects of her story have parallels today. She struggled with family loyalties, experienced hard times, and ultimately glimpsed the faithfulness of God. We may not be called to work in the fields like Ruth, but many of us will experience hard times in our lives — times when we need God's help.

1 Ruth's Commitment: costly decisions.

2 Ruth's Toil: God's faithfulness.

3 Ruth's Redeemer: our part in God's plans.

Ruth and her mother-in-law Naomi are the main characters in this story. To set the scene, split the group into two:

Group 1 Imagine you are Naomi — you have left your husband and your two sons to die, leaving you alone in a foreign country with your daughters-in-law, Orphah and Ruth.

Group 2 Imagine you are Ruth — you are a Moabitess married to a foreigner, your husband dies leaving you alone with Naomi and Orphah. Naomi decides to return to her homeland as the famine there is over. Naomi tells you to go and make your own life.

Each group asks ❑ How do you feel about your situation? ❑ What is your relationship with God like? ❑ How do you view the future?

Now join with the other group and discuss your responses.

IM

That we may take a serious look at our own family loyalties and learn from Ruth's example what God can do if we let him. (It is worth remembering that Ruth was the great grandmother of King David!)

Ruth's Commitment

Read Ruth 1:8-22. Three women face up to tragedy in different ways. The passage teaches us about the nature of commitment when life is difficult.

1 *Verse 13* What was Naomi's response to events that had overtaken her? Have you had times within your family life when things seemed hard? How did this affect your Christian life?

2 *Verses 10, 18 and 16* The two daughters-in-law made different decisions. What do you think influenced them? How committed are we to our close family — do we give up on those we find difficult?

3 *Verse 22* Bearing in mind Ruth left behind her home country and her own family and friends, what can her commitment teach us?

Discuss ▮

Can God ever expect too much of us?

Ruth's Toil

Read Ruth 2:1-3, 10-16 and 20. Ruth faces her need to work for a living and she encounters the faithfulness of God through a relative. We serve the same God today. What encouragement can we find in this story?

1 *Verse 2* It was a regular custom for the poor to glean the last of the harvest as it was law that farmers should not reap right to the edges of the field. Working like this may have been difficult for Ruth as previously she would have been supported by her husband. What was Ruth's attitude?

What is our attitude to work, whether at home or outside? Do we work hard whatever we're doing, or only if it's a job we feel worthy of?

2 *Verses 11-16* How did God reward Ruth for her hard work and commitment? What does this show about God's interest in our everyday lives?

3 *Verse 20* Boaz's reaction to Ruth caused Naomi to praise God. Yet she also believed that, as a relation, Boaz had a responsibility to Ruth. What is our attitude to relatives in need, particularly the elderly?

Ruth's Redeemer

Read Ruth 3:1-18. Naomi encourages Ruth to seek Boaz's hand in marriage. The story teaches us about human initiative and responsibility as part of God's plan.

1 *Verses 6-13* How do you view Ruth's action? Do you see Ruth as a weak or a strong person when it came to obeying her mother-in-law's wishes?

2 *Verse 10-18* Have you ever experienced positions of authority? How do you match up to Boaz?

3 What sort of images does the term 'arranged marriage' conjure up in your mind? What are the merits of taking advice over marriage partners? What is the advantage of a marriage that is to some extent 'arranged'?

Prayer ▌

Pray for the strength, commitment and loyalty found so evidently in this story. Share personal needs and circumstances in which you look to God for help.

MARY, the MOTHER

of CHRIST

Luke 1 and 2

INTRODUCTION

Mary is the best known woman in the Bible and her story is told so often that it is easy to miss its significance. Whether we are parents or not, Mary's life shows that God can use us in unexpected ways.

1 Mary's Calling: God's guidance.

2 Mary's Comfort: encouraging one another.

3 Mary the Mother: the challenge of parenthood.

To help to understand Mary's situation, three people could read Luke 1:26-38, taking the parts of narrator, Gabriel and Mary.

AIM

That each member of the group will always be open to God's calling — however surprising or unexpected it may seem.

Mary's Calling

Read Luke 1:26-38. A heavenly messenger tells Mary that God has a unique plan for her. This passage shows us how God guides and reassures.

1 *Verses 29, 34, 38* Picture the scene.... You are engaged to be married and are busy making wedding plans when you are visited by an angel who informs you that you will bear a child out of wedlock. The child will be 'the Son of the Most High'.

How did Mary react? How would *you* have reacted? Share any experiences you have had when God has 'spoken' to you. How does God speak to us?

2 *Verse 34* Mary did not doubt God's message, she just wanted to know how it would happen. How easy do we find it to believe that God is in control of our lives *whatever* happens?

3 *Verses 36-37* What reassurance did Gabriel give to Mary that God's promise of a child was real? Share any ways God has ever confirmed plans for your life (relationships, career, church and so on).

Discuss

Despite Mary's special calling, she would still have been socially criticized and shunned. How easily do we judge by appearances? What is our attitude to those whose relationships seem a far cry from the standards we believe God expects?

Mary's Comfort

Read Luke 1:39-56. Mary visits Elizabeth. We learn about the support and encouragement we can give one another.

1 *Verses 39-45* Family played a very important part during Mary's difficult circumstances. What did Mary gain from her visit to Elizabeth?

2 Who do we look to for spiritual help?

- ❏ Partner
- ❏ Wider family
- ❏ Friends
- ❏ Home group
- ❏ Church leaders
- ❏ Others

3 Do our beliefs play a natural part in our family life? Or do we find it much harder to follow God's teaching in our own homes?

Prayer

Look at Mary's song in Luke 1:46-55. Pray together, using the first two verses of the song. Like Mary, praise God for being with us whatever our own state of mind. Also, share any needs in the group, remembering anything which may have arisen from the study.

Mary the Mother

Read Luke 2:1-52. These verses relate the circumstances surrounding the birth of Jesus. We also see an incident where the behaviour of the young Jesus puzzles Mary and Joseph. There is a message here about the challenge of parenting.

1 *Verses 1-20* Not only had God called Mary to bear a child out of marriage (verse 5), but she had to give birth in unpleasant surroundings (verse 7). From these verses, how do you think God reassured her that he was with her and that this really was the Son of God?

2 *Verse 19* 'But Mary treasured up all these things and pondered them in her heart.' How often do we make space for ourselves to think and pray about what God is doing in our lives and those of family and friends?

3 *Verses 21-40* Joseph and Mary followed the biblical law and had Jesus presented in the temple at Jerusalem. We may not follow this tradition, but as parents or godparents how diligent are (were) we in following God's path for our children when they were young?

4 *Verses 41-45* There was obviously a great sense of community about this annual trip from Nazareth to Jerusalem with a group of relatives and friends all travelling together. Do we see our local church as a warm, welcoming family?

5 *Verses 46-52* It must have been a very puzzling experience for Joseph and Mary to find Jesus in the temple (verse 50), yet he returned home with them and 'grew in favour with God and men' (verse 52). What lessons can we learn from Joseph and Mary?

PRISCILLA

Acts 18:1-8 and 18-28

INTRODUCTION

Priscilla may not be the best known woman in the Bible but her appearance in both Acts and Paul's letters reveals an adventurous woman, faithful to the Lord. Her lifestyle will be familiar to many: a worker, a traveller, and a devoted follower of Christ.

1 Priscilla's Fearless Spirit: openness to change.

2 Priscilla's Ministry: witnessing through word and deed.

3 Priscilla's Hospitality: sharing her home.

Someone in the group may like to set the scene by reading the following:

'Priscilla and her husband were both Jewish Christians originally living and working in Rome as leather workers and tent makers. In AD 49 they were forced to leave Italy after a decree banning all non-Roman citizens. They travelled to Corinth in Greece where they met Paul. They later accompanied Paul on his missionary journey to Ephesus. Later, possibly following the death of Emperor Claudius and subsequent relaxations towards the Jews, they returned to Rome. They evidently continued to travel. The last mention of them is in Ephesus.'

AIM

That everyone in the group will come away with a fresh challenge in their lives, however big or small, inspired by the example of Priscilla.

Priscilla's Fearless Spirit

Read Acts 18:1-8 and 18-23. Priscilla and her husband encounter the apostle Paul in Corinth. Later they accompany him on his mission to Syria. Their example teaches us about willingness to be uprooted in order to fulfil God's purposes.

1 *Verses 1-4, 18-19* Imagine you have been asked to research some background material on Priscilla for a TV interview. From these verses, what facts would you come up with about her life? How would you describe her to the interviewer? Each member of the group may like to find a different 'label'.

2 *Verses 2, 18-19* Priscilla and her husband travelled thousands of miles, stopping only where God wanted them to be. Have members of the group ever been called to serve God away from home? Share your experiences of what it was like.

3 If you have always been based at home, how would you cope leaving behind friends and familiar environment if you felt God was calling you (and immediate family) to work for him abroad?

4 Is there a danger that we can accumulate so many possessions that we find it too hard to 'move on' for God?

Priscilla's Ministry

Read Acts 18:24-28. Priscilla and her husband play a vital part in bringing Apollos to know Christ. From this passage, we learn about sharing our faith and suffering for it.

1 *Verse 26* Priscilla and Aquilla showed no fear or embarrassment in their witness to Apollos and were able to explain the gospel clearly.

As a group, discuss practical ways to help

❏ those who are less confident to share their faith.

❏ young Christians who want to grow in their faith.

2 Should sharing the gospel be more than a matter of sharing the right Bible verse?

Discuss

Read Romans 16:3-5. Paul mentions how Priscilla risked her life for him. Not much is known of this incident. But from what we read of Paul and other New Testament leaders, persecution was a common experience.

Think of our own personal situations—at home, at work, in our social and church lives. Are we ever called to suffer for Christ today?

Priscilla's Hospitality

Read Acts 18:1-3 and 1 Corinthians 16:19. Meeting in people's homes was a regular feature of the New Testament church. We can learn from the early Christians' hospitality.

1 Priscilla and her husband not only provided a meeting place for the church in their home (this was probably very time consuming), but also opened their house to Paul while he was in Corinth. Could you be this hospitable? How do you react to having short- or long-term guests in your home?

2 Look at Romans 12:3 and 1 John 3:17-18. What lessons can we learn about hospitality from the New Testament?

Prayer ▌

Read Philippians 2:5-8, and then lead into a time of prayer. Remember the different needs and challenges that have arisen from the study.